MINING IN
CORNWALL
1850-1960

Volume One

J. H. Trounson
on behalf of the Trevithick Society

Moorland Publishing

© J.H. Trounson, 1980

Published 1980 by
Moorland Publishing Co Ltd
ISBN 0903485 79 6

This edition published 1985 by
Dyllansow Truran,
Trewolsta, Trewirgie,
Redruth, Cornwall
ISBN 0907566 83 9

Printed in Great Britain by
A. Wheaton & Co Ltd, Exeter

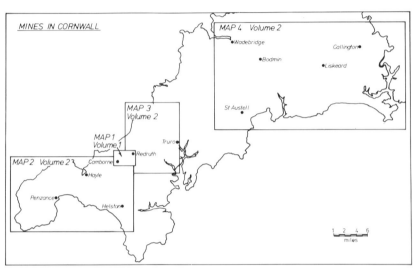

MINES IN CORNWALL

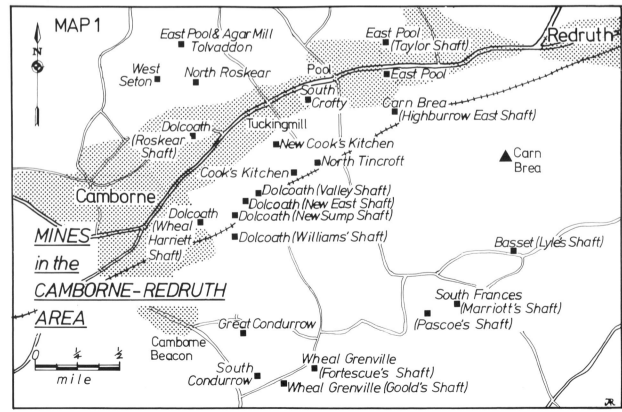

Introduction

IT has been said that a mine is a hole in the ground with a Cornishman at the bottom. This is a fitting tribute to the generations of Cornishmen whose labours have built up the Cornish mining industry of today, and whose skills are a byword in mining camps the world over. Traces of mining work may be found in almost every parish in the county, whether as buildings, shafts, adits or machinery. Buildings and machinery are particularly vulnerable in times of change, and it is thus of particular interest to publish the cream of a collection of photographs of mines, collected over the past half-century and spanning a period of over a hundred years.

Mining in Cornwall goes back to between 1,000 and 2,000 BC, and exploration for minerals has been undertaken over the centuries wherever they were thought likely to occur. The early workings were for tin, washed from the gravels in the beds of streams or dug from the shallow deposits which could be worked as open pits. Underground mining as we know it today is not thought to have started before the sixteenth century, when lodes cropping out on the cliffs around St Just began to be explored. As the workings went deeper other metallic minerals of economic importance were found, and the sixteenth century saw the early attempts to raise copper ore in the St Just, St Ives and Perranzabuloe areas. Mining for copper began on a large scale in the second half of the eighteenth century, and in terms of output reached its peak about a hundred years later. After about 1860 a decline set in, and by the end of the century the output of copper ores was negligible. Other minerals produced from the mines of Cornwall included arsenic, lead, zinc, wolfram, silver, nickel, cobalt, bismuth, ochre, sulphur, barytes and fluorspar.

The history of the mining industry in Cornwall in the past two hundred and fifty years can be said to be the history of the pumping-engine, since without suitable pumps mines cannot be worked. Early shallow workings were drained by pumps driven by waterwheels, and it was not until the early years of the eighteenth century, following the introduction of the steam pumping engine by Thomas Newcomen, that steam power began to be used for pumping mines. James Watt's improvements were a great step forward, but further development of the steam-driven pumping engine was inhibited by Boulton and Watt's patents: when these ran out in 1800 there began a steady period of development and improvement which continued until steam power reached its peak towards the end of the century. In the last seventy years steam has been entirely replaced by electricity for mine pumping.

Tin and copper ores formed the bulk of Cornwall's mineral output over the centuries. In very general terms shallow tin deposits gave way to copper in depth, and sometimes the copper was followed at still greater depth by major deposits of tin. The methods employed in mining the two ores underground was the same: adits were driven to carry off the water, shafts were sunk on the lodes to give access to the mineral deposits, and the lodes were broken and the ore was brought to surface. Once tin ore was raised from a mine it was ground to a powder by a crushing mill or by stamps. Nowadays there are numerous types of crushers in use, the so-called ball mill being based on a Cornish invention of the last century. The crushed ore was carried by water to a series of devices or machines which divided it into different sizes and separated the wanted material from the worthless waste or gangue, thus producing the valuable concentrate of tin oxide, locally known as black tin, which contains about two-thirds of its own weight of metal. This was then bagged and sent to the smelter. Until about fifty years ago tin was smelted in Cornwall. Copper ore, by contrast, was broken down into lumps about the size of a walnut, and in this form was sold to the smelters. Much of the work of breaking the ore at surface was done by hand by gangs of women and girls known as 'bal-maids'. After several attempts had been made to smelt copper in Cornwall in the seventeenth and eighteenth centuries copper ore was shipped to South Wales, where the smelting works had easy access to the large quantities of fuel needed.

Until after the end of the Napoleonic wars most mines in Cornwall were financed by the local business community and by the larger landowners. Then, as mines became deeper and were worked on a larger scale, capital began to flow into the county from London and the cities of the Midlands and North, notably from Manchester, Liverpool and Birmingham. Many of the sources of capital were the owners of manufacturing or smelting businesses, who needed to ensure a steady supply of raw materials for their own works, or who were persuaded that they might make a profit by speculating in mining shares.

In the coastal mining areas miners often combined their activities with fishing and farming. In the summer months, when there might be insufficient water for dressing the ore, a miner could be engaged in any one of a dozen occupations, including building, labouring, or growing crops for his family's consumption. In the St Just area mining was a popular occupation in the 1840s, since a miner was regarded as a skilled craftsman (he still is), and enjoyed a superior social status. Besides having a shorter working day than the labourer on the surface, a skilled miner could rise up in the industry to become a mine manager or a member of a mine's management committee. A successful speculation in mining shares might lay for him the foundation of a fortune and for his family a better standard of living.

The benefits to the county of a prosperous mining industry were numerous. Besides ensuring direct employment for thousands, the mines provided employment in the industries ancillary to mining, since they were buyers of large quantities of coal, timber, steel, iron, machinery and lubricants, much of which was bought from local merchants or foundries. These in turn needed finance and services, and so banking and transport prospered as mining activity rose. The booms and slumps in base-metal prices, which reflected the balance between supply and demand for metals, were an unavoidable risk for the highly risky mining industry, and, from time to time nearly brought mining in Cornwall to a halt. The slump of the 1890s led to the closure of all but a handful of mines, and spurred mining companies on to seek for better ways of conducting their operations, so as to ensure their survival. This led, too, to the abandonment of the time honoured system of working mines by partnerships with unlimited liability, and to the adoption of limited liability in its stead. It is perhaps worthy of note that two of the best mining companies at work in Cornwall today were started just over seventy years ago at a time of great technological change, and have survived thanks to their constant search for better methods and the adoption of the best ones.

This first volume deals with the highly mineralised area in the Camborne and Redruth area, while the second volume illustrates the mines in the remaining areas of Cornwall.

Justin Brooke

Camborne-Redruth Area

Lying on the slopes of the granite hills of Carn Brea and Carn Marth, this mineralised zone is about 3½ miles wide and 4 miles long. It contains more large mines than any other mining area of Cornwall, and has for centuries been regarded as the centre of mining in the county. Besides its many mines also located here is the world-famous Camborne School of Mines, formed at the end of the last century by merging several smaller establishments. On the northern slopes, from west to east, lie Dolcoath, Cook's Kitchen, Carn Brea and Tincroft, South Crofty, East Pool and Agar, North Roskear, West Seton, South Roskear, and many other mines. Beneath the southern slopes of the granite ridge is the Great Flat Lode, which was mined in South Condurrow Mine, Wheal Grenville, the Basset Mines, and other important concerns. Most of these mines were started for copper, but they found that in depth the copper gave way to tin. Records of these enterprises before the eighteenth century are scanty, though it is known that Tolcarne Mine, in the hamlet of that name, near Camborne, was at work in the 1580s. Much of the waste from the dressing plants of the mines in the Camborne-Redruth area was discharged into the Red River, and on its way to the sea was treated by numerous tin streaming plants.

1

1 By the turn of the century the once very productive South Condurrow Mine, south of Camborne, was nearing exhaustion but was kept drained by the neighbouring Grenville Mines. A part of South Condurrow was therefore taken over by the Camborne School of Mines in order to provide its students with invaluable practical instruction. Subsequently this was re-named the King Edward VII Mine. The powerful steam-driven Cornish stamps for crushing the ore at South Condurrow was not required by the School of Mines and was later taken over by the adjacent Great Condurrow Company when their mine was reopened in 1906.

2 When it was decided to unwater the old and deep Great Condurrow Mine, situated on the high ridge of ground south of Camborne, the decision was taken to do the work through Woolf's Shaft. As the collar of the shaft had collapsed, leaving a large cone-like cavity, the first thing to do was to cover this over and make preparations to put in a new concrete collar. This picture shows the work in progress, early in 1906.

3 The building of the new engine-house at Woolf's Shaft at Great Condurrow, 1906. The first part of the permanent headgear has been erected and the small one beneath it is being used for the work of reconditioning the shaft down as far as the adit or drainage level which is here at the unusually great depth of 300ft from the surface.

4

4 Woolf's Shaft, subsequently renamed Neame's (after the Company's Chairman), when the machinery was in operation, about 1912. From left to right, the new winding engine, the large boiler-house containing five large Cornish boilers, and the fine 80 in diameter cylinder Cornish pumping engine. The shaft proved to be a very crooked and dangerous one requiring heavy timber to make it secure and the Company expended most of its capital in dealing with it, only to find that the old workings were very poor and largely blocked by debris. The whole thing was a very ill-conceived venture and the mine closed down again in 1913. Although now roofless, the big engine-house still stands and is a prominent landmark visible from a considerable distance.

5 In April 1897 the chimney stack of the large pumping engine at the Fortescue's Shaft of Wheal Grenville, south-east of Camborne, was struck by lightning, doing considerable damage to the engine house as well as to the stack itself.

6   The deeper part of Fortescue's Shaft at Wheal Grenville was sunk on an incline and this photograph is believed to have been taken in this shaft, probably early this century. It shows the heavy Cornish pump parts including the great moving wooden 'main rod' running on rollers, as seen towards the right-hand side of the picture. This massive wooden rod was attached to the outdoor end of the cast-iron beam of the pumping engine and reciprocated in unison with the engine stroke.

7 The principal 'lode' or mineral vein of the Grenville and Basset group of mines was one dipping at a very shallow angle and known as The Great Flat Lode. This photograph shows miners at work in this lode. One miner holds and turns the boring bar, while his partner strikes it with a two-handed hammer.

8 The Old Cornish stamps at Wheal Grenville, one of two there which crushed the tin ore, and driven by the rotative beam engine with its twin flywheels.

9 In September 1906 the great cast iron bob or beam of Goold's Shaft pumping engine at Wheal Grenville broke in the centre, doing considerable damage to the other parts of the engine. A replacement 38-ton beam was cast by Holman Bros Ltd of Camborne, but so great was the mass of metal in the two castings that they were too hot to touch for a fortnight after casting! In the picture one side of the new beam can be seen up in place, while the other side is being lifted.

7

8

9

10 The repairs to Goold's pumping engine having been completed it is here seen at work again with its new bob.

11 Marriott's Shaft pumping engine at South Frances Mine after the house had been gutted by fire in the early hours of Monday 9 December 1895.

12 At about the time of the fire at Marriott's Shaft, the South Frances Mine together with the neighbouring Wheal and West Wheal Basset Mines were amalgamated to form the Basset Mines Ltd. Marriott's Shaft became the principal producing one of the group and the whole of the plant there was replaced and the shaft itself enlarged and deepened. The 80in diameter steam cylinder of the old Cornish pumping engine was used as the low-pressure cylinder of a new inverted compound, high-pressure beam engine, the only one of its type to work in Cornwall. This photograph shows Marriott's Shaft with the new plant completed and in operation about 1910. From left to right, the ore bin and rock crusher station, the buildings containing the crusher and steam capstan engine, air compressor, pumping engine, high-pressure boilers and big conical-drum winding engine.

13 An interior view of the compound pumping engine showing the 40in high-pressure cylinder on the left, which took steam at a pressure of 150lb/in^2, and on the right-hand edge of the picture, the 80in low-pressure cylinder. The beam was under the floor.

14 The original steel-plate beam of Marriott's compound pumping engine was of inadequate strength and began to break up. After an unsuccessful attempt at patching, it was decided to have a new and stronger beam in 1909 and this is seen in the builder's works at Motherwell in Scotland. At 55 ton weight this was the largest and heaviest engine beam to work in Cornwall.

15 Marriott's Shaft as viewed from the north showing, from left to right, the central boiler-house, the pumping engine and air compressor buildings. The old plate beam of the pumping engine (awaiting scrapping) can be seen just left of centre of the picture, taken about 1910.

16

16 A group of miners about to go underground at Marriott's Shaft of the Basset Mines, about 1910. Note the candles stuck in a lump of clay and attached to the men's hats — the conventional means of illumination in the Cornish mines in those days. The neatly dressed man on the right of the group is the winding engine driver. The small boy in cap in the centre of the group is *not* one of the miners!

17 As Marriott's Shaft was a considerable distance from the two ore dressing plants of the Basset Mines a narrow gauge railway system was constructed to connect them. To haul the trains of wagons a small steam locomotive was purchased. The German firm of Orenstein and Koppel were prepared to supply the necessary engine, complete with copper fire-box, for £400, whereas the lowest English quotation was £800, so the German firm got the order. The picture shows the little locomotive at the side of Marriott's winding engine house about 1910.

18 The 80in cylinder pumping engine and beam winding engine at Pascoe's Shaft of the Basset Mines about 1910.

19 The Old Stamps at the Bassett Mines photographed early this century. The rotative beam engine which drove these stamps was a very unusual one consisting of two engines joined together to make a double cylinder engine with cranks arranged at 90 degrees to one another thus making for easy starting as well as being a very powerful unit.

20 A rather rare photograph taken early this century showing two Cornish type boilers working at the Basset Mines with a third one under repair, and the brickwork of the flues surrounding that boiler partially stripped to facilitate the repairs.

LYLE'S ENGINE. BASSETT MINES.

23 The stamps engine at North Roskear Mine to the north of Tuckingmill, photographed late last century. This was a great and profitable copper mine which also produced some tin. After the mine closed down the stamps were in use for several more years for crushing dumps and other lesser sources of tin from the surrounding old mines. The unusual castellated house and chimney with gothic window openings were supposed to be less offensive to the eye of a large local landowner whose house was about a mile and a half distant and who derived a very large annual income from mineral royalties paid to him by the mines.

24 The only known picture of the famous West Seton copper and tin mine, north of Camborne, which was highly profitable in its day, photographed sometime before it closed in 1891. The stamps engine can be seen on the left-hand side of the picture and Michell's Shaft and its pumping engine on the right. Note the secondary beam driven from the stamps engine to work a small pump to provide water for the dressing and crushing floors.

21 Tin dressing 'floors' at the Basset Mines with some of the women or 'bal girls' employed in the work in the olden days.

22 Lyle's Shaft with its 80in cylinder Cornish pumping engine at the eastern section of the Basset Mines early this century. At the right-hand side of the picture a part of the old beam winding engine (then only used for working the capstan drum for lifting heavy pump parts in the shaft) can be seen. The more modern winding engine was out of sight beyond the waste dump. The large building abutting the pumping engine house contained the Cornish boilers.

23

24

Cook's Kitchen Mine

This mine lay east of Dolcoath Mine and west of Tincroft Mine. There is a tradition that it was opened by a man named Cook, who described its main lode as being as wide as his kitchen. The mine is thought to have been at work in the 1690s, and although it was working in 1766 nothing is known of its earlier history as the agents ('captains') of the mine burned nearly half a ton of its old documents about 1844. The mine paid no dividends from 1809 to 1854 — surely a record — and the shareholders celebrated its return to the dividend list in the latter year by presenting a gold watch to its manager, Captain Charles Thomas, a first cousin of Josiah Thomas, the famous manager of the adjoining Dolcoath Mine. The mine was divided in the latter part of the nineteenth century, the northern part being worked as New Cook's Kitchen. This was closed during the slump of the 1890s and reopened as part of South Crofty Mine early this century. The southern part was amalgamated with Carn Brea and Tincroft Mines in 1895 and, in common with the other members of the group, was finally closed in 1913.

Dolcoath Mine

The earliest records of this mine show that it was being worked for copper in 1740, and probably earlier. It was nearly 300ft deep in 1746, and an extensive mine in 1778, when a section of its eastern part was published in Pryce's *Mineralogia Cornubiensis*. It closed ten years later, to reopen in 1799. In the next 120 years it became the largest and deepest mine in Cornwall, with its bottom level 3,000ft below the surface. Its output of copper and tin ores to 1788 is thought to have been not less than £1,250,000, of which copper alone realised some £450,000 between 1740 and 1777. Between 1799 and 1920 its output amounted to over £9 million, including income from sales of arsenic, silver and other minerals. The mine was in the dividend list for most of its working life, and its shares, nicknamed 'Dollies', were the 'blue chip' of the industry.*

* Further information can be found in *Dolcoath, Queen of Cornish Mines*, by T. R. Harris, published by the Trevithick Society.

25　The Camborne and Illogan mining district as viewed from the western side of the Tuckingmill Valley, about the commencement of the twentieth century. In the foreground are the eastern surface works of the great Dolcoath Mine with its Valley Shaft in the centre of the picture on the far side of the valley. Beyond the top of Valley headgear and slightly to the right are the engine houses of Cook's Kitchen Mine clustered around Chappel's Shaft; this is one of the deepest mines in Cornwall. On the right-hand side of the picture is the rugged granite hill of Carn Brea, with its monument and castle, which overlooks the scenery of the area. In this photograph there are at least thirty-three mine chimneys and thirteen engine houses.

26 A very old photograph of Cook's Kitchen Mine taken from near the bottom of the Tucking-mill Valley. It was said of that mine in 1893 that 'It has certainly been working without a day's suspension for 150 to 200 years' and as it did not close down until 1913 it must be one of the oldest mines in Cornwall. It was very productive of both copper and tin ores and was highly profitable in its earlier years. Near the left-hand side of the picture is the early sinking headgear on the Valley Shaft of the Dolcoath Mine, while in the foreground is a large group of round buddles for dressing the ore.

27 An old type of compressed air winch working at the 406 fathom level of Cook's Kitchen Mine when Chappel's Shaft was being further deepened in 1893. The winch is raising broken rock in an iron kibble which then loaded into waggons.

28 New Sump Shaft at Dolcoath, Cornwall's deepest and richest tin mine, probably about 1893. This shaft, for many years the principal one of the mine, ultimately reached a depth of a little more than 3,000ft; its historic pumping engine dated from 1815. A piece of the 'bob' or beam with the date cast on it has been preserved by the Trevithick Society.

27

28

29 This picture shows the new steel headgear then recently erected on the New Sump Shaft at Dolcoath in 1896, with remains of the old wooden one lying on the ground. To the right is the headgear of New East Shaft and the old beam engine which had previously wound from both these shafts.

30 When the New Sump pumping engine was built it had a steam cylinder 76in diameter but when the mine became very deep this was of insufficient power and the engine was rebuilt with an 85in cylinder. This occupied so much space in the house that there was inadequate room for the stairs and a unique wooden structure was added to the back end of the engine house as shown in this photograph.

31 Men and 'bal-girls' at Dolcoath, breaking rocks and shovelling the stuff into carts while carpenters repair the low gantry on which small rail waggons ran from New East Shaft, loaded with ore, again photographed in the late nineteenth century.

32 A group photographed before going underground at Dolcoath Mine. The central figure, sitting on the wheel, is believed to have been Oliver Wethered, Vice-Chairman of the Dolcoath Company, and behind him is Captain William Thomas, a well-known mining man of those days. The other two men are obviously visitors! In the background can be seen the winding drum and flywheel of Old Sump beam winding engine, a most economical machine which worked until the closure of the great old mine in 1920.

33 Dolcoath men (especially the standing figure on the right) and visitors who have already been underground, to judge from the dirt on their whiteduck suits.

34 Dolcoath miners riding on the Man Engine at the 234 fathom level in 1893. Note the candle burning on each man's hat. The man engine was a means of ascending and descending the mine by stepping on and off the platforms of the reciprocating engine rod. The photograph also shows the splendid width and typical inclination of the Dolcoath lodes or mineral veins.

32

35 A 'stope' at the 375 fathom level of Dolcoath in 1893, where the ore has been mined and a tram road above has had to be hung in chains after a heavy fall of ground, or a 'run', had damaged some of the timber.

36 The massive timbering or 'stull' at Dolcoath's 412 fathom level (2,400ft from surface) where the lode was very wide and exceedingly rich. Unfortunately, this place was the scene of a terrible accident shortly after the photograph was taken in 1893. In consequence of a heavy fall of rock the massive timbers collapsed and seven men lost their lives. An eighth man was rescued unhurt after thirty-seven hours' entombment, his escape being truly 'marvellous'.

36

WORKINGS IN DOLCOATH MINE

37 It is not known in which Cornish mine this photograph was taken, but it shows men working on a stull of more normal dimensions and forms an interesting contrast to the immense stull at the Dolcoath 412 fathom level.

38 A powerful horizontal air compressor at Dolcoath whose house stood at the eastern end of Dolcoath Avenue, photographed early this century.

37

38

39

40

39 A general view of the surface works at the central section of Dolcoath, as it appeared early this century. From left to right: New East Shaft headgear, the central crushing station (partly hidden by steam), New Sump winding engine and the headgear on New Sump Shaft, the historic pumping engine with its square stack, the building with tall arched windows containing the big vertical air compressor and (partly hidden by steam) the headgear on Old Sump Shaft. On the right-hand edge of the photograph is Wheal Harriett Shaft and pumping engine.

40 A close-up view of the two larger stamps engines at Dolcoath, seen late last century. The stamps themselves were under the cover of the long wooden sheds. This was an unusual refinement in Cornwall where the employees, known as 'stamps watchers', were expected to brave the weather. Both these rotative beam engines have a secondary beam to power small pumps.

41 In the Tuckingmill Valley, the three Dolcoath Cornish stamps batteries and the mass of tin-dressing equipment, only partly covered by rough wooden sheds. Dolcoath was originally a great copper mine, indeed it was the fifth largest copper producer in Cornwall and Devon, of which there were altogether about 470 mines both big and small. As depth increased at Dolcoath the copper died out and was replaced by tin. Between 1853 and 1920 this wonderful old mine produced a little over 100,000 tons of 'black tin' or tin oxide — by far the largest output of tin from any of the 400 or so mines in Cornwall which produced that metal.

42 A group of 'bal maidens' at Dolcoath who helped to 'dress' or prepare the ores. Large numbers of women were employed in this way on all the Cornish mines in the past. This is very much a posed photograph as all the women have put on their clean white aprons in which they would travel to and from their work. As soon as the photograph had been taken the white aprons would be replaced with rough hessian ones for the rough and dirty work as the ores were often red and muddy.

43 The 'Dry' or change house at Dolcoath where the miners could wash and exchange their wet and dirty underground clothes for their surface clothes and the wet ones were then dried over hot pipes. In its day this was regarded as very advanced accommodation for the employees for in olden times, and in the case of smaller mines, the miners often had to walk long distances to their homes in wet underground clothes! This shows

the dry probably soon after it was built in 1888, with the underground clothes hung up to dry over steam heated tubes down below.

44 Wheal Harriett Shaft and pumping engine at Dolcoath Mine about 1896, after the erection of the new steel headgear and before the old wooden one had been taken down.

45 Some of the Dolcoath shareholders gathered together at one of their meetings. The group includes several men who were famous in their day and who made a considerable impact on the mining and associated industries of the late nineteenth and early twentieth centuries, both at home and abroad.

46

47

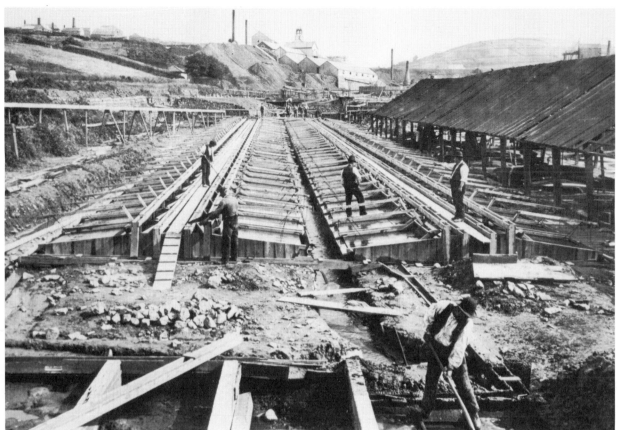

46 A large group of Dolcoath miners about to go underground at Valley Shaft with the 'lander' or banksman in a white coat and bowler hat in the foreground. Most of the men have their candles fixed on their hats or in their hands, or hanging from their jackets.

47 The Directors of Dolcoath Mine Limited on the occasion of the cutting of the first sod of the famous 3,000ft Williams' Shaft on the 26 October 1895. The top-hatted figure in the back row is Captain Josiah Thomas, the Managing Director, and the gentleman holding the engraved silver shovel is Mr Michael Henry Williams, JP, the chairman of the company who performed the ceremony of cutting the first sod. To mark the occasion each man employed by the company received two shillings (now 10 pence) and each boy and 'girl' (ie woman) one shilling as a present! A photograph taken at the time shows the great crowd of employees, then believed to have been about 1,300, gathered together in their best clothes in front of the Count House. Following the ceremony at the site of the new shaft the shareholders partook of a luncheon where a number of speeches were made. One of the agents or mine captains stated that he wished the shaft was down instead of just started for it would, when completed, effect a vast saving in the working expenses of the mine, as at that time it took the men employed in the lower levels from 2 to 3 hours to go down and come to surface, consequently they did not work more than 4 to 5 hours a day.

48 New 'rag frames' being made by Dolcoath Mine carpenters in the Tuckingmill Valley for catching more of the very fine 'slime' tin escaping from the existing dressing plant, probably early this century. In the central background of the picture can be seen the then new type of Californian stamps of Dolcoath, the first of the type to be erected in Cornwall and, above the stamp buildings, the headgear of Valley Shaft.

49

50

51

52

49 A heavy Lancashire-type boiler being hauled to Dolcoath Mine by a large team of horses, as was common before the days of the steam traction engines.

50 After a very long and prosperous career the old Dolcoath Mine closed down in 1920 as it was by that time virtually worked out. In 1923 the company was reconstructed, fresh capital raised and a new 2,000ft circular shaft sunk far north of the old mine, at Roskear. The photograph shows the sinkers at work in the bottom of the new shaft, about 1924-5.

51 From a point about a mile south of Tuckingmill down to the coast at Gwithian where the Red River discharges into the sea, a distance altogether of about 6½ miles, the river valley was an almost continuous mass of 'tin-streaming' plants which extracted the very fine tin contained in the effluent flowing from the mines and which, for a variety of reasons, could not be caught by the mines themselves. One of the last of these tin streams to remain in operation was the plant at Tuckingmill owned by the Tolgus Tin Stamping Company and before it was dismantled in the winter of 1973-4 a number of photographs were commissioned for the Trevithick Society for record purposes. This picture shows a concave buddle for up-grading fine tin.

52 A round frame for treating very fine tin.

53

54

53 A set of round frames being dismantled.

54 A large bucket or elevator wheel for lifting mill pulp from one set of machines to others.

55 Also at Tuckingmill was Bartle's Foundry, where in 1941-2 parts were made for what was probably the last Cornish pump to be installed in a mine in any part of the world. This was for the Castle-an-Dinas wolfram mine near St Columb Major, in mid-Cornwall. Wolfram is the ore from which the vitally important steel hardening metal tungsten is obtained and which was in very short supply during World War II. The picture shows the valve boxes, etc, of this double 'pole' (or ram) Cornish pump assembled before being dispatched from the foundry.

South Crofty Mine

Shallow adits were driven into this mine in search of copper about the middle of the eighteenth century, though it seems likely that these were preceded by shallow workings for tin at some earlier date. From the 1830s the mine formed the southern part of East Wheal Crofty, and was separated from it in 1854, its northern boundary running along the main road from Redruth to Camborne. To the west it included old mines such as Longclose, Dudnance, Copper Tankard and Wheal Susan, and various boundary adjustments were later made with the neighbouring mines. Operations came to an end in 1896 when base-metal prices were very depressed, but three years later a new company was formed to work the mine with New Cook's Kitchen, and operations were resumed early in this century. In July 1906 the concern was converted into South Crofty Limited, and the mine is still at work today.

56

56 A very old photograph of unknown date of the original part of the South Crofty Mine at Pool. It shows, from left to right, the old single-cylinder horizontal winding engine, Palmer's Shaft and pumping engine, Bickford's Shaft and, seen faintly under the tramroad bridge spanning Station Road, the mine Count House, now the South Crofty Company's office. The old thatched roof cottage is believed to have been the birthplace of Richard Trevithick, the great Cornish engineer and inventor who gave the world the steam locomotive.

57 In 1906 the old South Crofty mining company was reconstructed and further capital raised to enable new perpendicular shafts to be sunk, new plant installed and the whole mine entirely modernised. This photograph was taken at the time the lofty new headgear was being erected on Robinson's Shaft. Unfortunately, the pumping engine made a stroke at the moment the photograph was taken and hence the bob is blurred.

57

58

59

58 A later stage in the erection of the new headgear and ore bins at Robinson's Shaft.

59 Foundations for the new winding and air compressor engines at Robinson's Shaft, with two large Lancashire boilers already in place. On the left in the mid-distance can be seen Palmer's old shaft and pumping engine of South Crofty Mine. In the far distance and at the foot of Carn Brea Hill can be seen the engine-houses of Carn Brea Mine.

60 The erection of the new plant at Robinson's Shaft in an advanced state.

61 The new plant around Robinson's Shaft nearly completed and seen from the east.

62 Robinson's new headgear and rock breaker plant in operation with a train of waggons filled with ore on the way to the mill, possibly about 1909-10.

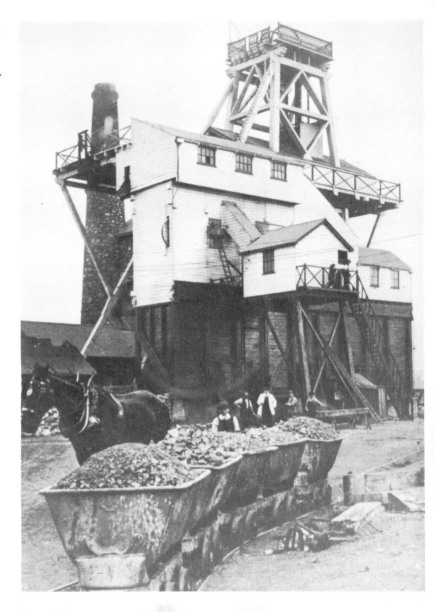

63 South Crofty's old steam-driven Cornish stamps early this century.

64 A close-up view of the old Cornish stamps at South Crofty with the new stamps being erected on the far side of the engine-house, about 1907. The cams which raise and drop the heavy stamp heads and so crush the ore can be seen clearly.

65 The new Californian stamps and concentrating tables at South Crofty during erection about 1907.

66

66 The then new steam winding engine at Robinson' Shaft built by Holman Brothers of Camborne and replaced many years later by an electrically driven machine. This steam engine was a very fast one.

67 Robinson's Shaft in the 1950s as it appeared after the wooden headgear had been replaced by a steel one. This photograph gives a fine view of the famous old 80 in cylinder pumping engine which appears in another picture when working at the Tregurtha Downs Mine near Marazion. It was erected at South Crofty on the then new Robinson's Shaft in 1903 and finally ceased working there in its 101st year on Sunday 1 May 1955 when its duty was taken over by the new electrically driven pumps. It was the last Cornish beam pumping engine to work on a Cornish mine and is now in the care of the National Trust.

68 Amongst the new machinery installed at South Crofty when the mine was reconstructed in 1906-7 was a new small steam winding engine at Palmer's Shaft at the eastern end of the mine. This photograph, taken from the top of the pumping engine house, shows the new winder working in the open with only a temporary shelter over the driver while the new house was being built around the engine. On the far side of Station Road can be seen the massive sand 'tailings' dumps which had accumulated from the working of the Carn Brea and Tincroft Mines over more than half a century.

These dumps were later removed and re-treated for their tin content with the aid of more efficient machinery. The site is now partially occupied by the Carn Brea Leisure Centre. In the upper right-hand corner of the picture Martin's East Shaft and Willoughby's Shaft of Tincroft Mine can be seen.

69

69 The concession of the new South Crofty Company included the New Cook's Kitchen Mine, then lying idle, where the Company had agreed with the mineral owner to sink a new perpendicular shaft. This picture shows the commencement of the shaft in 1907, which is now (1980) 2,420ft deep and is the main ore hoisting shaft of the whole mine. In the background can be seen the new South Crofty milling plant then under construction and, by its side, the old stamps engine, which was demolished shortly afterwards.

70 In 1921 a very heavy fall of ground destroyed the two hoisting shafts of the neighbouring East Pool and Agar Mines; pumping there ceased and a great volume of water then flowed into South Crofty Mine through workings where the two mines were connected. In order to prevent South Crofty being permanently flooded it became necessary to install a second powerful pumping engine and it was decided to place this on the New Cook's Kitchen Shaft as that one alone was large enough to accommodate the actual pumps in the shaft. This photograph shows the building of the new engine-house in 1922 to contain the 90in diameter cylinder beam engine which had been purchased from the Grenville Mines, then recently closed. For ease and speed of building it was decided that the engine-house should be constructed of heavily reinforced mass concrete instead of the conventional stone and the picture shows the work in an advanced state. The whole of this concrete was mixed by hand and it is estimated that about 7,800 tons of material went into the building, which was completed within about 5 months! As far as is known it was the only beam engine-house in the world built entirely of concrete with the exception of the brick arches over the window and door openings and the brick upper portion of the chimney stack.

71 The new pumping engine on New Cook's Kitchen Shaft in operation about 1923. Dismantling of the engine at Wheal Grenville, excavations for the foundations of the new engine-house (about 20ft deep) and preparations in the shaft for installing nearly 1,200ft of large 'pitwork' (the actual pumps) all commenced early in January 1922. The engine commenced working early in the following November — a good piece of work!

72 Every Cornish pump needs to have one or more 'balance bobs' to counterbalance the excess weight of the moving pump rods in the shaft. In the case of the very large pump in New Cook's Kitchen Shaft there was one balance on the surface and three more underground. The picture, taken about 1937, shows one of the latter before it was lowered down the shaft in pieces by the powerful steam capstan. This is historically interesting as it was the very last balance bob ever put down in a Cornish mine. The two men on the right, the brothers Jory (Jack with miner's hat and lamp, and Arthur with trilby hat) were the last of the great 'pitmen' of Cornwall who installed and maintained the world-famous Cornish pumps.

73 To prevent surface and 'shallow' water from making its way down into the deep workings, which greatly increases the working costs of a mine, South Crofty has wisely paid much attention in recent years to the overhaul and repair of the various adits, or

comparatively shallow drainage tunnels, that exist in its area. In order to do this it was necessary to have a small portable winding plant which could be quickly assembled at any one of numerous shafts where it became necessary to lower or raise men, materials and/or rock. A steam winch and boiler were therefore mounted on a steel framed chassis fitted with small

iron wheels which could be removed on reaching each site, and a small two-leg headgear was also made to complete the set. This photograph, probably taken in the 1950s, shows this most useful little equipment being assembled at one of the several sites where it was used and before the sectionalized shed had been erected over the engine and boiler.

74 At 5·45am on 28 December 1950, one side of the great 45 ton cast-iron beam of New Cook's Kitchen Shaft pumping engine broke in two and a piece weighing 7 tons crashed down on to the side of the shaft. Had it gone into the shaft untold damage could have been done. The photograph was taken as preparations were being made to lift the broken piece of metal so dangerously poised at the very edge of the shaft. The vapour appearing as smoke was the result of the warm moist air coming up the shaft condensing on meeting the cold air of a winter's day.

75 The broken piece of the beam being lifted by the steam capstan a few minutes after the previous photograph had been taken. At the top of the picture the stump of the broken side of the beam can be seen against the sky, with the other side still standing intact. There did not appear to be any flaw in the metal of the beam and the smash was undoubtedly due to the excessive weight being lifted by the engine, so that the beam was overloaded. The other parts of the engine were so damaged in the smash that it was not worth trying to make any repairs and temporary electric pumps were installed to limit, as far as possible, the flooding which resulted from this breakage.

76 The two Cornish pumps at South Crofty were working almost to the limit of their capacity and in view of the rising cost of coal the decision had been taken in principle to replace them with electrically driven pumps before the smash of New Cook's Kitchen engine occurred. Two large pump stations were therefore blasted out of the solid granite at the 195 and 340 fathom levels at New Cook's Kitchen Shaft and a fine set of centrifugal pumps installed therein. The picture shows the five pumps at the 195 fathom level (nearly 1,200ft below the surface) with the electric motors on the left and the pumps, in grey paint, down the centre, the switchgear being at the far end of the station, in the 1960s.

76

78

77 A miner at work at South Crofty with a stoping machine drilling an 'upper', or a near vertical hole, which will be charged with dynamite and blasted. This and the following fourteen photographs were taken during or just after World War II.

78 Loading a waggon from the main ore-pass chute at the 310 fathom level in Robinson's section of South Crofty.

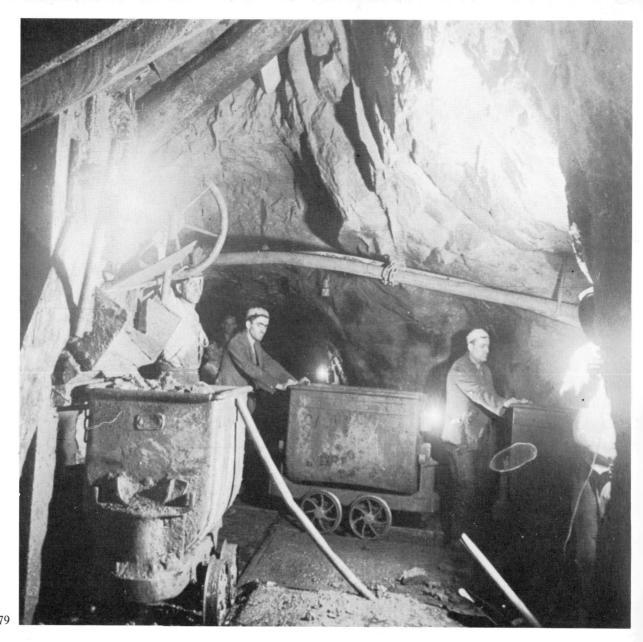

79

79 Trammers at work at the 310 fathom level in South Crofty Mine.

80 Loading a waggon with ore from a 'mill' or chute at South Crofty.

81 Trammers dumping waggon loads of ore onto a 'grizzley' at South Crofty. Any rocks too large to pass through the grizzley are broken with a large hammer held by the man on the left. This hard work is now done mechanically by underground electrically driven rock breakers, and most of the 'tramming' is now done by small electric battery or diesel loco-motives hauling trains of waggons instead of each being pushed by a man.

82 'Croust time', when a Cornish pasty tastes particularly good!

83 A cage load of men arrive on surface at Robinson's Shaft at the end of the shift.

84 The ore having been hoisted to surface at South Crofty Mine was crushed to a smaller size in rock breakers and then loaded into trains of narrow gauge waggons and hauled by horses or small diesel locomotives to the mill where it was crushed to a fine size. This rail transport on surface has now been superseded by rubber conveyor belts.

85 Miners at South Crofty washing and changing in the 'dry' after their return to surface. This primitive type of change-house has long ago been replaced by far better accommodation with proper showerbaths, etc.

86

87

6 The Californian stamps at South Crofty which crushed the ore to a fine size preparatory to it being treated on vibrating tables to separate the black tin or tin oxide from the waste material. The lifting cams should be compared to those on the old Cornish stamps (Fig 64). The stamps have now been replaced by rotary rod mills.

87 As a further means of upgrading the tin concentrate it was treated in rotary buddles. Although very effective machines for their purpose, buddles cost too much in labour for handling the material and have now been succeeded by other types of machine requiring far less labour to operate.

88 Digging out the heavy material from a 'dumb' buddle.

89 Stirring or 'tossing' the tin concentrate to up-grade it still further. This labour-intensive proceedure has now been succeeded by more economical methods.

90 Bagging up the precious (and very heavy) final high-grade tin concentrate before dispatch to the tin smelters who will produce from this brown powder the shining white metal of commerce.

91 In addition to the tin, the South Crofty ore contains smaller amounts of the sulphides of copper and arsenic etc. Hitherto the tin concentrates were roasted in these rotary furnaces or 'calciners' in order to eliminate the sulphides. With the rising cost of fuel this operation is now done more economically by the froth flotation process.

92 In the shallower levels of South Crofty the ore contained large quantities of arsenic which then commanded a good price. After the impure tin concentrates had been roasted in the calciners the arsenious oxide, which was driven off, condensed in labyrinthine brick chambers in the form of a grey powder known as 'arsenic soot'. This was again burnt with a smokeless coke/anthracite fuel in the refinery furnace to produce the pure snow-white arsenious oxide of commerce. The picture shows the arsenic soot on the upper floor of the refinery before being loaded into the refining furnace.

91

92

93

93 The refined white arsenic being shovelled into the grinding mill to reduce it to a fine powder. The mill was similar to an old-fashioned flour mill in which the grinding was performed by means of a large circular dressed stone revolving on top of a stationary stone. The small amount of stone dust produced did not seriously pollute the finished product as would the metal from any form of metallic grinding process.

94 The finely ground arsenious oxide descended through leather hoses and was packed in specially made paper-lined wooden barrels and, because of the highly poisonous nature of this substance, the barrels were sent away in locked railway vans. There is now virtually no demand for arsenic and it has ceased to be produced in Cornwall.

East Pool and Agar Mine

Started on the continuation of an adit begun early in the eighteenth century, the profits from which provided the Basset family with funds to build Tehidy mansion, East Pool mine took a new lease of life when a company was formed to work it in 1834. It was worked until 1784 as Pool Old Bal (bal being Cornish for mine), and then from 1834 to 1897; the mine joined with Wheal Agar in the latter year to become East Pool and Agar, a title which it retained after adopting limited liability in 1913. It was closed in 1945 following the refusal of the government to allow the company to raise the additional capital needed for the exploration and development of the eastern part of the mine. This work is now being undertaken by South Crofty Limited, which has taken over the area formerly worked by the East Pool and Agar company.

95

95   An old photograph of the principal shaft (Engine Shaft) at the East Pool Mine taken at about the turn of the century. On the left and in the distance can be seen the engine houses of Wheal Agar which was amalgamated with East Pool Mine in 1897. Although both mines were worked on the same series of lodes, whereas Wheal Agar was poor throughout the greater part of its history East Pool was extremely productive and highly profitable!

96 Michell's Shaft at East Pool Mine and its beam winding engine which was made in 1887 and, as such, was probably the last engine of its type built in the world. It was a very economical engine on coal, and it is now fortunately preserved and in the care of the National Trust. During the summer months of each year it can be seen in motion daily. A further interesting feature of this photograph, which was probably taken during the 1890s, is the curving rail supported on wooden posts in the foreground. This was a part of the electric Telpher mono-railway erected in 1890-1 in the expectation of being able to convey the ore from the mine to the company's mill, a distance of a mile and a quarter, more cheaply than was then being done by horses and carts. It was a system which showed great promise, but in practice it was not a success and only worked experimentally.

97

98

99

97 By the time that this photograph was taken early this century (as also were the following four pictures) a rock breaking plant had been erected at East Pool which enabled the ore from both hoisting shafts to be crushed mechanically in the building seen left of centre in the picture. Most of this area is now the site of Messrs Macsalvor's machinery yards.

98 A close up view of East Pool Engine Shaft with the engineer's fitting-up shop in the foreground.

99 Michell's Shaft and beam winding engine on the left, and East Pool Engine Shaft on the right of the picture. Michell's winding engine has fortunately been preserved and is now a familiar sight to passers-by on the A30 road at the top of Pool Hill.

100 East Pool Mine as seen from the A30 road. From left to right, Michell's Shaft headgear, the rock breaker plant, the Engine Shaft headgear, and the front of Michell's Shaft beam winding engine.

101

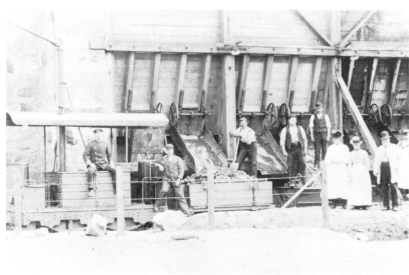

102

103

101 Michell's Shaft headgear and winding engine as seen from the east. The wooden shed in the foreground is covered with posters advertising the sale of furniture, boots and shoes, a hotel to let, etc.

102 In 1902 the Camborne and Redruth Tramways commenced to carry passengers between the two towns and in the following year the owners, the old Urban Electric Supply Co Ltd, contracted to haul the ore from the East Pool and Agar Mines to the company's mill at Tolvaddon, a distance of about a mile and a quarter. The little mineral trains used the same track as the public

passenger carrying trams along the A30 road to the top of Tuckingmill East Hill and then branched off on a purely mineral line to the discharge point at Tolvaddon. The picture shows one of the mineral trains loading from the ore bins under the rock breakers at East Pool with two of the bal maidens looking on.

103 East Pool pumping engine and the Engine Shaft with its peculiarly shaped headgear, as viewed from the east, about 1907-10. In the centre is the back of the rock breaking plant with rejected big rocks which were found to be too large to go into the rather small crushers. When blasted and broken up, these rocks were shown to carry payable tin values. On the right-hand edge of the picture, the now-preserved beam winding engine on Michell's Shaft and part of the face of a man (out of focus) who was standing too close to the lens of the camera!

104 The mineral train consisting of an electric locomotive and four loaded waggons leaving East Pool for Tolvaddon, sometime after 1903.

105 An underground bridge at East Pool Mine at the 170 fathom level (1,130ft from the surface) in 1893.

106 The Wheal Agar Mine about 1907-10. From left to right, the rock breaker house, the derelict engine-house on the old Agar Engine Shaft, the new Agar Engine Shaft and the winding engine. The smoking stack on the extreme left of the picture is that of the East Pool pumping engine on the south side of the Camborne-Redruth road.

107

107 The new Wheal Agar Engine Shaft with its massive 90in diameter cylinder Cornish pumping engine — one of the largest ever to work in Cornwall — probably photographed in the second decade of this century. The all-granite house with its unusual narrow slit windows and clock in the top storey was a notable feature on the north side of the Redruth-Camborne main road.

108 The extensive milling and tin dressing plant of the East Pool and Agar Mines at Tolvaddon in the Tuckingmill Valley. The little electrically hauled ore trains ran along the wooden viaduct seen against the skyline and discharged their loads into the large building beneath the smoking steel chimney. On the extreme right of the picture can be seen one of the two big arsenic calcining chimneys which were demolished at the time of building the Camborne-Redruth by-pass road. At the bottom of the picture is the Red River on its way to the coast at Gwithian.

109

109 A row of concentrating tables in the East Pool and Agar mill at Tolvaddon.

110 In May 1921 an extensive fall of ground occurred in the workings of the old part of East Pool Mine and both winding shafts were destroyed. It then became necessary to sink a new shaft to the north of the old workings in order to resume production. The new Taylor Shaft, named after the then manager, was commenced in January 1922. The picture shows the small sinking headgear on the shaft and the big 110ft chimney stack on the day that it was completed, with the masons standing on top of it. The white letters built into the red brickwork stand for 'East Pool (and) Agar Limited', EPAL being the trade brand of the company's arsenic which it produced in very large quantities in addition to tin at that time.

111 The permanent headgear on the new Taylor Shaft has been erected, the winding engine and air compressor houses completed and the building of the Cornish pumping engine-house commenced; the large granite quoins are being lifted with the aid of a temporary crane fixed in the headgear. In the foreground can be seen the massive cylinder bottom and cylinder cover of the great pumping engine which was erected when its house had been completed. A scene in 1923.

112 At the Taylor Shaft the walls of the pumping engine-house are up and ready for the roof, and the rock-breaker station is in an advanced stage of construction. Large steam pipes and parts of the pumping engine are lying in the foreground.

113

113 The 90in diameter steam cylinder of the pumping engine, with its outer steam case (25 tons in all), after arriving from the Carn Brea Mines for re-erection at the Taylor Shaft of East Pool & Agar Ltd. The late M. T. Taylor, the manager, after whom the shaft was named, is in the centre of the group. On the left is Captain Dick Gilbert and on the right Captain Tom Grose.

114 The 52½ ton beam, made by Harvey & Co Ltd at Hayle in 1892, was one of the heaviest cast-iron bobs ever made for a Cornish pumping engine. The length of this great beam is 33¼ft between centres and the weight of each side is 24 tons. The piston stroke is 10ft and the stroke of the pump rods 9ft. The total weight of the engine was stated at the time of building to be 125 tons. The engine was purchased second-hand from the nearby Carn Brea Mines and hauled to East Pool by two large traction engines, one of which can be seen above the bob. The big cylinder can also be seen in the background. This engine has the distinction of being the last pumping engine erected in Cornwall and was one of the last to work, its duty not being taken over by electric pumps until 1954. It was preserved by the Trevithick Society and has now been placed in the care of the National Trust and is visited by great numbers of people every year.

115 The Taylor Shaft believed to have been photographed on VE Day in 1945 with the flag flying to celebrate the return of peace after the end of World War II.

90 INCH PUMPING ENGINE AT TAYLOR'S SHAFT, EAST POOL MINE

116 In or about 1928 a new tin smelting process was undergoing trial and a new mobile furnace was built which could be moved from mine to mine to try it out on different grades of tin oxide. The first experiment was at East Pool Mine where the heavy part of the rotary furnace can be seen just after its arrival, with the Taylor Shaft in the background. In spite of prolonged experimenting the process was not a success and this heavy plant was ultimately cut up at what proved to be its first and only stopping place!

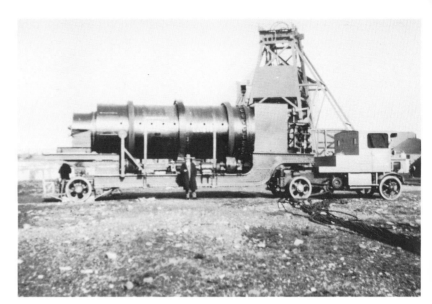

117 The Camborne and Redruth Tramway which commenced to run in 1902 finally succumbed to bus competition in September 1927 and the track was later removed, but the section between East Pool and Tolvaddon remained until the mineral trains also ceased to run in August 1934. A new mono-cable aerial ropeway was then brought into commission to convey the ore directly across country to the mill. This picture, taken in 1934 from the upper part of Taylor's pumping engine-house, shows the ore bin and loading station of the ropeway with one of the buckets being filled with broken ore (on the left-hand side of the picture, and in the shadow of the bin.) This ropeway was a very economical and satisfactory system and continued to operate until the mine closed down in 1945.

118 Notwithstanding the installation of underground dams between the new and old parts of East Pool Mine after the old shafts had collapsed, it was feared that the amount of water to be pumped in future by the Taylor Shaft pump might be more than the plant could handle. As there was insufficient room in the new shaft in which to install a second Cornish pump, a big electrically driven four-throw pump was ordered. The picture shows it assembled in its maker's works in 1923, but though it was delivered it was

never required and remained in store on the surface for over 20 years. It was ultimately sold to the South Crofty Company but it did not fit in well with their major new electrical pumping scheme and was finally scrapped without having pumped a single gallon of water!

119 A now out-dated type of diamond drill at work in the Taylor Shaft section of East Pool Mine, about 1939.

119

120 Early in 1923 Tolgus Mines Ltd, a company associated with East Pool and Agar Limited, commenced the sinking of a new deep shaft to the east of the latter company's mines with a view to opening up their lodes nearer to Redruth. The photograph was taken on the occasion of the cutting of the first sod of the new shaft by Capt Algernon H. Moreing, MP (holding the ceremonial shovel). The central figure is Dr Malcolm Maclaren, the geologist, and to the right, with hat in hand, Captain M. T. Taylor the manager of East Pool and Agar after whom the Taylor shaft was named.

120

121

121 In 1896 the Carn Brea and Tincroft Mines amalgamated. In their earlier days they had been very productive and profitable but they were not a success after the amalgamation; with the exception of the North Tincroft section they were all closed down in 1913. This photograph shows a group of visitors about to go underground at Carn Brea with the manager, Captain W. T. White, the black-bearded figure by the skip. The date is probably some time in the 1890s. Note the wonderful hat of the old lander (or banksman) on the left!

122 'Door pieces' or valve boxes of the Cornish pump in the deep Highburrow East steeply inclined shaft at Carn Brea Mines, in the 1890s. The moving 'main rod' of the pump is the large baulk of timber in the centre of the picture.

123 Old Crusher Whim at Tincroft in the mid-1920s. This was so named because the beam engine also drove Cornish rolls for crushing the copper ore (in the square building on the left) as well as the winding drum by the side of the big flywheel. 'Whim' is the Cornish term for any form of winding machine. Note the square chimney stack which was very unusual in Cornwall and probably dates from quite early in the nineteenth century. In the background can be seen Harvey's Shaft 70in cylinder pumping engine on the South Tincroft section of the mine.

124 When the Carn Brea and Tincroft Mines closed in 1913 it was feared that as those workings flooded, other mines in the area would be affected through per- colation. A number of mining companies and mineral royalty owners therefore combined to reconstruct the pumps in the Highburrow East Shaft at the Carn Brea Mines so that the powerful engine there could, pumping from a lesser depth, handle all the water previously pumped by four engines from a greater depth. This photograph, taken, it is thought, in 1915 shows the work of installing the new pumps. Unfortunately, for a variety of reasons the co-operative pumping arrangements broke down in about 1917 and the big engine remained there idle until purchased by the East Pool and Agar Company for their new Taylor Shaft.

125 The North Tincroft Mine must have been the most old- fashioned one in Cornwall when it closed down at the time of the great slump in 1921. The photo- graph shows Tyrie's Shaft and its small and ancient pumping engine and, in the background, the 'North' Cornish stamps engine. In a short-lived revival of mining at Tincroft in the 1920s, when it was worked mostly for arsenical ore, the North stamps worked again and when it finally stopped in 1926 it was probably the last steam- driven Cornish type of stamps to work anywhere in the world.

126 An old-time scene at Tincroft Mine with men and bal girls breaking rocks with the 'surface captains', or bosses in white duck coats.

127 Buddles and other machines in the old-fashioned tin dressing floors at Tincroft Mine.

128 A magnetic separator at Tincroft for removing wolfram and other magnetic particles from the tin concentrates, probably in the early 1920s.

128

129 Round frames at Tincroft for catching the fine or 'slime' tin.

129

Index